On the Go
Motorcycles in Action

David and Penny Glover

PowerKiDS press.
New York

Published in 2008 by The Rosen Publishing Group, Inc.
29 East 21st Street, New York, NY 10010

First Edition

Editor: Camilla Lloyd
Editorial Assistant: Katie Powell
Designer: Elaine Wilkinson
Picture Researcher: Kathy Lockley

Picture Credits:
The author and publisher would like to thank the following for allowing these
pictures to be reproduced in this publication:
Cover: Ducati (both); Bubbles Photolibrary/Alamy: 8, Lourens Smak/Alamy:
9, TNTMagazine/Alamy: 11b, Joern Sackermann/ Alamy: 14, Mike
Greenslade/Alamy: 15, Martin Jenkinson/Alamy: 19, Colin Woodbridge/Alamy:
21; Patrick Bennett/Corbis: 7, Torlief Svenson/ Corbis: 2, 10, Gene Blevins/LA
Daily News/Corbis: 11t, Alain Nognes/ Corbis: 12, Reuters/Corbis: 13, Matthias
Hiekel/epa/Corbis: 20t, Pascal Rossignol/Reuters/Corbis: 20b; Ducati: 1, 4, 18;
Kawaski: 6; Popperfoto. com: 22; Rex Features: 16t, 17; Nigel Dickenson/Still
Pictures: 5; Suzuki: 16b.

Library of Congress Cataloging-in-Publication Data

Glover, David, 1953 Sept. 4-
  Motorcycles in action / David and Penny Glover.
      p. cm. — (On the go)
  Includes index.
  ISBN 978-1-4042-4311-8 (library binding)
  1. Motorcycles—Juvenile literature. I. Glover, Penny. II. Title.
TL440.15.G62 2008
629.227'5—dc22

                                            2007032448

Manufactured in China

Contents

What are motorcycles?

Motorcycles are vehicles with two wheels and an **engine**. The rider sits on top of the motorcycle. Motorcycles are fun to ride. They are smaller than cars and use less **fuel**.

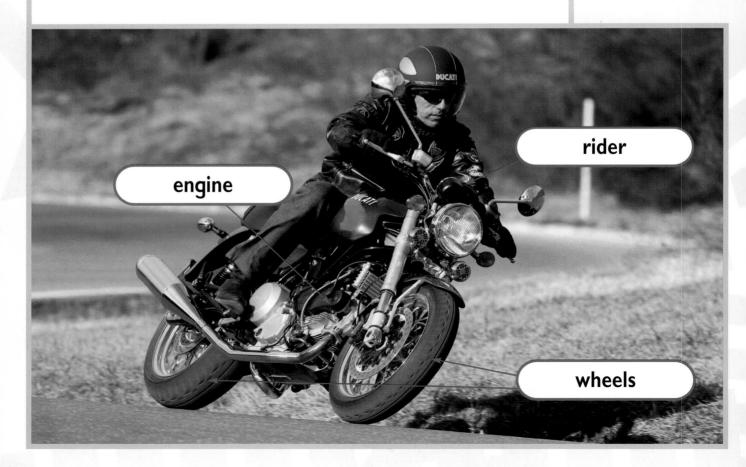

rider

engine

wheels

Motorcycles can travel on roads and tracks. This farmer uses his motorcycle to find his sheep in the fields.

sheep

Motorcycle quiz
How many wheels does a motorcycle have?

Motorcycle parts

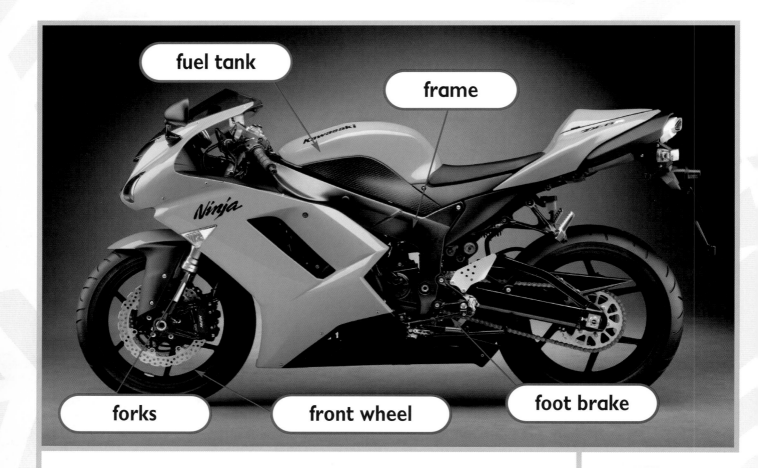

fuel tank

frame

forks

front wheel

foot brake

The motorcycle's engine is fixed to a strong **frame**. The rider sits above the engine, behind the fuel tank. The **forks** fix the front wheel to the bike. They turn so the rider can steer the bike.

The rider holds the **handlebars** to control the bike. He turns the **throttle** to speed up, and squeezes the **brake** to slow down. The **speedometer** shows how fast the rider is going.

brakes

speedometer

handlebars

throttle

Motorcycle quiz
How does the rider make the bike speed up?

What makes it go?

The engine makes the motorcycle go. It needs **gasoline** to make it work. The rider fills the tank with gas at the gas station.

The motorcycle is like a bicycle, but instead of the rider pedaling, the engine does the work.

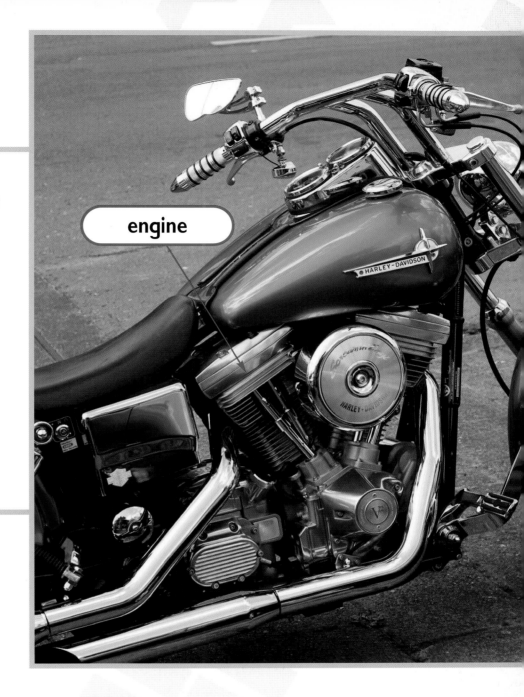

engine

Motorcycle quiz
What does the engine need to make it work?

Working motorcycles

Police motorcycle

The police bike is powerful and fast. Flashing lights and a loud noise warn people when it is speeding to an emergency. Some police officers ride Harley Davidson motorcycles.

Firefighting bike

Some firefighters ride motorcycles, too. On crowded city streets, a firefighting bike is faster than a fire engine.

Delivery bike

These bikes deliver pizza. They are quick and easy to park, so the pizza arrives hot!

Motorcycle quiz
What make of motorcycle do some policemen ride?

Scooters

mirrors

step-through frame

A **scooter** is a motorcycle
with a **step-through frame**.
Scooters are light and easy to ride.
They are good for city travel.

These police officers in Brazil are riding electric scooters. Electric scooters are quiet and do not make **fumes**.

electric scooter

Motorcycle quiz
What kind of frame does a scooter have?

Quad bikes

Quad bikes have four wheels instead of two. A quad bike's thick tires let it cross soft ground where a motorcycle would get stuck. Quad bikes are "All Terrain Vehicles," or **ATVs**.

handlebars

seat

thick tires

A lifeguard uses a quad bike to patrol the beach. The thick tires are good for driving on sand.

Motorcycle quiz
What is an ATV?

Record breakers

Special motorcycles called **Streamliners** are the fastest in the world. They can only go in straight lines.

The Suzuki Hayabusa is the world's fastest road motorcycle. It can reach 200 miles per hour.

This is one of
the smallest bikes
in the world.
It is called the
pocket bike.

Motorcycle quiz
What is the fastest
road bike?

Riding safely

Riding a motorcycle is more dangerous than driving a car. Riders must always wear **crash helmets** and leather clothes to protect them if they fall off.

crash helmet

leather clothes

Before you can ride a motorcycle, you must pass a test. New riders learn how to control their motorcycles at a riding school.

Motorcycle quiz
What must you do before you can ride a motorcycle?

Motorcycle fun

Motorcycles take part in races and displays. Grand Prix races are the fastest. The riders lean to the side to speed around the bends.

Motocross races are on rough, bumpy tracks. The dirt bikes fly through the air at the tops of hills.

Motorcycle display teams do tricks and stunts. The riders must practice to make their stunts safe.

Motorcycle quiz

What kind of track do motocross bikes race on?

Old motorcycles

Motorcycles have changed over the years. This is the first motorcycle with a gasoline engine. It was made more than one hundred years ago. Its top speed was 8 miles per hour.

Motorcycle words

ATV
All Terrain Vehicle: a vehicle that can go on any kind of ground, not just smooth roads.

brake
The part of a motorcycle that slows it down.

crash helmet
A strong, hard helmet that every motorcycle rider must wear to protect their heads.

engine
The part of the motorcycle that makes it go.

forks
The parts that fix the front wheel to the frame.

frame
The main part to which all the other parts of the motorcycle are fixed.

fuel
Something that burns inside an engine to make it work.

fumes
Dirty clouds of smoke that some engines give out.

gasoline
The fuel most motorcycles use to make them go.

handlebars
The part the rider holds and turns to steer the motorcycle.

pocket bike
One of the smallest motorcycles.

quad bike
A vehicle like a motorcycle but with four wheels.

scooter
A motorcycle with a step-through frame.

speedometer
The part that shows the rider how fast the motorcycle is going.

step-through frame
The low frame of a scooter that makes it easy to ride.

Streamliner
The fastest bike in the world. It only travels in straight lines.

throttle
The part of a motorcycle that speeds it up.

Quiz answers

Page 5 Two.

Page 7 By turning the throttle.

Page 9 Gasoline.

Page 11 Harley Davidson.

Page 13 A step-through frame.

Page 15 An All Terrain Vehicle.

Page 17 The Suzuki Hayabusa.

Page 19 Pass a test.

Page 21 Bumpy tracks.

Index

Web Sites
Due to the changing nature of Internet links, PowerKids Press has developed an online list of Web sites related to the subject of this book. This site is regularly updated. Please use this link to access this list:
www.powerkidslinks.com/otg/motoract